TENDERS OF THE SACRED FIRE

Sermons For
Pentecost (First Third)
Cycle A, First Lesson Texts

R. ROBERT CUENI

CSS Publishing Company, Inc.
Lima, Ohio

TENDERS OF THE SACRED FIRE

Copyright © 1995 by
CSS Publishing Company, Inc.
Lima, Ohio

Some scripture quotations are from the *New Revised Standard Version of the Bible,* copyright 1989, by the Division of Christian Education of the National Council of the Churches of Christ in the USA. Used by permission.

Some scripture quotations are from the *Good News Bible,* in Today's English Version. Copyright (c) American Bible Society 1966, 1971, 1976. Used by permission.

Library of Congress Cataloging-in-Publication Data

Cueni, R. Robert.
    Tenders of the sacred fire : sermons for Pentecost (first third) : cycle A, first lesson texts / R. Robert Cueni.
      p.   cm.
    ISBN 0-7880-0450-6
    1. Bible, O.T. Genesis—Sermons 2. Pentecost season—Sermons. 3. Sermons, American. I. Title.
BS1235.4.C84   1995
252'.6—dc20
                                          95-12289
                                            CIP

This book is available in the following formats, listed by ISBN:
0-7880-0450-6 Book
0-7880-0451-4 IBM 3 1/2 computer disk
0-7880-0452-2 IBM 3 1/2 book and disk package
0-7880-0453-0 Macintosh computer disk
0-7880-0454-9 Macintosh book and disk package
0-7880-0455-7 IBM 5 1/4 computer disk
0-7880-0456-5 IBM 5 1/4 book and disk package

PRINTED IN U.S.A.

To Bucky as he joins the family.

Table Of Contents

Foreword

"Which of your statues is the greatest?" someone asked the famous Danish sculptor, Bertel Thorvaldsen. "The next one!" he replied.

Most pastors feel that way about their sermons. No matter how effective the last one, its success was not permanent. Sunday is coming.

Bob Cueni's sermons help pastors address that never-ending opportunity/challenge. (It often feels like an opportunity on Monday and a challenge on Saturday.) His preaching meets the unspoken criteria most pew residents bring to a church sanctuary: 1) biblically rooted, 2) easy to understand, 3) tells me something about myself that I feel God wants me to know, and 4) encourages me to believe that I can apply this truth to my life.

Great preaching does more than illuminate the truth about the Bible. Great preaching illuminates the truth about life, with light from the Bible. Cueni hits that target in insightful ways. His communication style evokes the highest praise pulpit residents can give their peers: "That will preach!"

A cartoon character standing before a gathering said, "Before I begin to speak, I'd like to say something." The people who show up in Christian buildings on Sunday morning hope to hear the pastor say something *after* he or she begins to speak. The sermons in this volume can increase the likelihood of that happening.

Herb Miller
Lubbock, Texas

Preface

This book is a collection of sermons based on the Revised Common Lectionary from Pentecost 1 (First Third). With the exception of the first, which is a reading from the book of Acts, the lessons are from Genesis and concern primeval history or the patriarchs. I have titled the collection after the first sermon, *Tenders Of The Sacred Fire*. This refers to that spark of faith that was passed by the ancients through the generations until it burst into the Sacred Fire of Pentecost. Each successive generation has tended that fire and passed it along until it was entrusted to this present generation. Our responsibility is to tend it, stoke it and pass it to those who will follow us.

Obviously, many people have made this book possible. I am indebted to my wife Linda. She is always the first to read a sermon manuscript. Her comments, suggestions and support have undergirded my ministry for nearly a quarter of a century and my life for more than 32 years. Georgene Swank graciously gives of her editorial skills each week by preparing the written copies of my sermons that are distributed to the congregation and radio audience. Particularly, I am indebted to the staff and membership of the Country Club Christian Church in Kansas City. They not only know that " 'Country Club' is the name of our neighborhood; it is not our mission statement," but also they struggle with me in trying to discern God's will for the Third Millennium for this great congregation.

Wrestling with these texts has been a joy. Human nature and the workings of God in our world simply have not significantly changed in the past few thousand years. Consequently, these ancient stories overflow with relevant insights.

Pentecost
Acts 2:1-21

Tenders Of The Sacred Fire

Today is Pentecost, the day of the Sacred Fire. It was less than two months since the crucifixion of our Lord. The apostles and other followers of Jesus still spent most of their time in a borrowed room in Jerusalem. They were still too frightened to tell their story to the world. They were waiting for something to happen. They believed somehow God would give them a message of what to do and then give them the strength to do it. They sincerely believed Jesus was to return and usher in the Kingdom of God.

It was the Jewish festival of Pentecost, so named because it fell 50 days after Passover. Jerusalem was crowded with tourists and religious pilgrims. With all the activity in the city, the followers of Jesus were probably even more frightened than usual. After all, if not openly persecuted by the holiday crowd, they certainly would be ridiculed.

Then something happened which changed their lives and our lives. As we read the account in the book of Acts, it is obvious Luke cannot find adequate words to describe the event. "And suddenly from heaven there came a sound like the rush of a violent wind, and it filled the entire house where they were sitting. Divided tongues, as of fire, appeared among them,

11

and a tongue rested on each of them" (Acts 2:2-3). It was nothing less than the power of the living God, the Holy Spirit, coming into the midst of the followers of Jesus.

It is important to note that while Luke has difficulty wrapping mere words around the Holy Spirit in order to show us a recognizable shape, he speaks clearly about the result of the coming of the Holy Spirit. These terrified followers of Jesus were transformed into courageous witnesses of the Christ. From men and women too frightened to appear on the city streets, these people were transformed by the coming of the Holy Spirit into fearless preachers willing to sacrifice their lives. Peter, the apostle who denied he even knew Jesus on the night of the Master's arrest, took his stand on the curb of a Jerusalem street and preached a sermon so convincing that 3,000 people were converted to the cause of Christ.

These were the events of the day of Pentecost, the birth day of the Church of Jesus Christ. It is the day God entrusted the tending of the Sacred Fire of the Gospel to the people. The fire burned brightly in Jerusalem that day. But it was not God's intent for this Sacred Fire to stay there. By the power of the Holy Spirit, the followers of the Christ spread the fire to the whole world. It was first taken from Jerusalem to the Palestinian hills of Judea and on to Samaria. In only a few years it spread through Asia Minor to Antioch of Pisidia, Pergamum, Smyrna, Ephesus, and Galatia. In a dream to the missionary Paul, God gave the word to take the fire of faith to Europe. The Sacred Fire of the faith began to burn in Corinth, Athens, Philippi, Thessalonica and on to Rome, capital of the empire. The apostles tended the fire carefully and passed it to those who were not apostles. The first generation passed it to the second generation. The second generation passed it to the third and they tended it for the fourth.

In less than 100 years the Sacred Fire of the Gospel of Jesus Christ was carried as far as Spain to the west, India to the east, and Ethiopia to the south. It took several hundred years for the Sacred Fire to arrive in the northern reaches of Europe, but it did. Down through the centuries the flames of the Fire burned brightly. The Christian faith gained and its ranks grew because people who were attracted to the Sacred Fire had their lives changed. When people were filled with the power of the Holy Spirit, they came to know that peace that passes all understanding. The followers of Christ were known to demonstrate enormous courage under duress. Roman authorities tried to stamp out the Church by persecuting those who claimed Christ as Savior. The plan backfired. Those who were torn apart by wild animals in Roman arenas for the entertainment of the emperor and his entourage faced their deaths so courageously that others were attracted to the faith rather than repulsed by it.

The early church quickly gained standing as faith communities where people treated one another differently. "See how they love one another" was a well-deserved reputation that attracted people to the church. The caring character of Christians showed itself particularly in the treatment of the sick. Disease, plague, and epidemic were commonplace. The population of a city could be devastated by an untreatable infectious disease. The ordinary citizenry frequently became so threatened by pestilence that they abandoned their sick, when elementary nursing care might have saved them. Christians were different. Their commitment to Jesus Christ translated into the religious duty to care for the sick and dying. And for that matter, the teachings of the faith made the life of the Christian meaningful even in the midst of surprising and sudden death.[1] Those who adhered to the Christian faith founded hospitals and orphanages and schools and established a myriad of other social agencies. People noticed how the Christian faith could turn a person's life around; how the faith moved people to treat one another in love; how Christians seemed to be motivated to get involved making a difference in the world; how people in the Church of Jesus Christ seemed to demand the best of themselves and the world around them. Uncounted millions were attracted by the light when the Sacred Fire burned brightly in the Church of Jesus Christ.

At other times the Sacred Fire was reduced to a glowing ember of what should have been. There have always been those who get the message twisted. Too many times people have killed one another in the name of Christ. There has always been a smattering of corrupt religious leaders and terrible injustices perpetrated and preserved in the name of the faith. Unfortunately, not everything done in the name of Christ or by His Church has been just, beneficial or even moral.

Yet in every generation there have been committed people, saints of the church, who faithfully tend the Sacred Fire of the Good News of what God did and continues to do in Jesus Christ. Eventually, Christian people brought the Sacred Fire to the shores of the New World. There were Congregationalists in Massachusetts, Catholics in Maryland, Calvinists in New York, Anglicans in Virginia. The Sacred Fire of the faith was carefully tended and taken from generation unto generation until it was brought to this town and to this street corner.

A spark flashed in this community. A faith community was born and the flames quickly spread through this neighborhood. The charter members knew, of course, that they were doing something that must continue beyond the founders of the congregation. As George Hamilton Combs put it, "What we begin, others will complete. The good is like the building of cathedrals. Only through faith can those who lay foundation stones hear bells ringing in unraised steeples."[2]

Each pastor has taken a turn as lead tender of the Sacred Fire for the building of this cathedral. And now the fire has been handed down to us. We must tend it carefully and prepare to hand it to those who will follow. The task is probably no greater for us than for any other generation, but mark this: We cannot take the future of our congregation for granted. Enormous challenges confront Christ's Church today. All around us we see the evidence of the trivializing of religion in general and Christianity in particular in America. In his book, *The Culture Of Indifference,* Stephen Carter builds an outstanding case for the fact that religious belief and practice

14

are excluded from serious public discourse in America; that we treat religious faith as if it is nothing more than some sort of optional hobby; that, as a nation, we seem to have forgotten that strong religious institutions are mandatory safeguards against the intrusive power of state into our lives.[3]

A case can be made that the flames of the Sacred Fire do not burn as brightly as they did in the 1950s. And this is happening at a time when the nation faces a serious spiritual crisis. We see the symptoms all around us. We think the problem has something to do with education, but it is a spiritual crisis that is at the root of schools graduating students who cannot read. It is a spiritual crisis, not a sociological phenomenon, that is at the root of families falling apart because people cannot maintain lasting, respectful relationships between husband and wife, between parents and children. We think it has to do with politics, but at its root it is a spiritual problem that government has nearly ceased to function because of gridlock and that the citizenry really believes it can fund the functions of government through state-sponsored gambling. It is a serious spiritual problem when the fear of crime is never far from our every waking thought. And certainly it is our spiritual crisis at the root of the fact that the nation is so racially divided we are terrified of those who are different.

As the church, we need to address this crisis of the human spirit with the good news of the Gospel of Jesus Christ. We are tenders of the Sacred Fire of faith. We need to continue to build here a community of faith which is concerned to reach out to this neighborhood, to this city, to the world. To do that, we will probably need to find new ways to be the church. The present generation does not necessarily want to do things exactly as the last generation. In fact as one of the foremost congregational consultants puts it, "the big issue is change."[4] The congregations that make the necessary changes to reach the present generation are those that will be strong enough to pass the flame to the future.

Having said that, I also need to say that the most important things will never change. We need to maintain here a church that is concerned to be a place where people can experience the presence of God. We will do that in our relationships with one another. Fellowship has always been essential to the practice of our faith. We will also do that in the hearing of the Word of God. In the study of the scripture, in the preaching of the Word, in the hearing of sacred music, people have always caught the fire of faith.

On this Pentecost Sunday, we celebrate the birthday of the Church of Jesus Christ. It is a time we remember and give thanks for those who have tended the Sacred Fire of our faith and have passed it down through the generations. It is also a time for us to pray the continued presence of the Holy Spirit that we will have the courage and strength to tend this fire and pass it to the next generation. And may we come to the end of our watch being able to say what Combs said, "What we begin, others will complete. The good is like the building of cathedrals. Only through faith can those who lay foundation stones hear bells ringing in unraised steeples."

_____

1. William McNeill, *Plagues And People*, (Garden City, New York: Anchor Books, 1976), p. 108.

2. On the chapel wall of Country Club Christian Church, Kansas City, Missouri.

3. Stephen L. Carter, *The Culture Of Disbelief,* (New York: Basic Books, 1993), pp. 3-23.

4. Lyle Schaller, *Strategies For Change,* (Nashville: Abingdon Press, 1993), p. 10.

Holy Trinity
Genesis 1:1—2:4a

The Essence Of Spirituality

Our scripture for today comes from the first words of the first book of the Bible. We probably best know it as the seven-day account of creation. By way of orientation, let us remember that this is Holy Writ and not an article from *The Journal Of The American Academy Of Science.* As such it embodies a statement of our faith. While science has its place in our lives, this is not it. Frankly, science has a very narrow boundary on what it accepts as truth. It can describe the facts very well, but seldom, if ever, does science capture the full *meaning* of an event. Science does its best job with the physical, but it does not have the tools to capture the essence of the human spirit. Remember, a good scientific definition of a kiss is "the exchange of bacteria between the anterior ends of two digestive systems." While accurate in all the facts, this definition does not encompass the full weight of a romantic kiss between two people who passionately care for one another.

The Bible, on the other hand, shows us a way to see through eyes of faith and to focus on the meaning of existence. This creation passage from Genesis is particularly important because everything else in scripture flows from it. It proclaims that God and God's creation are bound together in a very distinctive way.[1]

17

Biblical scholars broaden our understanding by observing that this first account of creation comes from the time of the exile in Babylon. It underscores the orderly and caring ways of the Lord God at a time when life seemed incoherent and cruel.

Nothing in this account is casual. As each verse is turned in the light, meaning after meaning reflects from facet after facet as understanding moves from deep unto deep. It speaks of God's sovereignty over the forces of chaos and evil; of God's blessing in the gift of life; of God's assurance of persistent concern for people; and of God's expectation that the human species will be blessed as we both use and take responsibility for the earth and all that is in it.

Stated succinctly, this passage proclaims the goodness of creation. The orderliness surrounding us did not result from a random jumble of disconnected accidents. The world came into being and continues in existence as an act of God's love. Our lives are not the result of capricious and random forces intent on nothing more than trapping us in an empty existence. God created the world and God created us. All around us, through eyes of faith, we see the evidence of this. As we come to understand that truth and live in the midst of that truth, our lives are empowered.

Gary Marsh is an Olathe, Kansas, physician who participates with other physicians who give of their time, energy and material resources to help the poor in developing countries. In a recent interview he spoke not only of his commitment to medicine, but to the Christian faith. He commented that he struggles with really important questions, like "Why are we here?" and "What is the purpose of life?" In his estimation, "to ask these things is to be a spiritual person."[2]

Indeed the essence of spirituality is to know we are in the midst of a world created by God. As the old spiritual puts it, "He's got the whole world in his hands. He's got the little baby in his hands. He's got you and me in his hands. He's got the whole world in his hands." Knowing that and living as though it is true empowers and enriches life. Rabbi Michael

Zedek offers a powerful image from the Jewish mystical tradition. "Imagine," he writes, "the only thing there is ocean. That means, of course, that there are waves. And waves by definition are part of the ocean before they become waves, while they are waves and after they go back *into* the ocean."[3]

Rabbi Zedek goes on to explain that we might compare the ocean to God, the ground of being out of which we all come. Each wave then might be thought a person. We come into being and for a brief time we have our chance in the sun, then we sink back and become part of the ocean again. That fits well with our faith which teaches us that life is eternal. By definition, eternal means without beginning and without end. Like the water within the ocean which forms the waves and then returns to the ocean, we come from God and return to God.

It needs emphasized as well that because every wave comes from the same ocean, all waves are connected to one another. They are of the same substance. In that way, every one of us are connected. We all come from the same God and return to the same God. We are part of one another. Indeed, He's got the whole world in his hands. Knowing that and living as though we know it is the essence of spirituality.

For a moment, let me use a different analogy to demonstrate a different facet of this truth. Consider what it takes to hang a heavy object on the wall. In order to secure a large, framed painting, a random nail through the plaster board will not do the job. Any heavy object will pull the nail out of the soft board. Underneath the wall, however, are 2x4's, spaced about 16 inches on center. You cannot see them, but they are there and they hold up the wall, indeed they hold up the house. When you put the nail through the wall and into the 2x4, it holds. As with all analogies, we should be careful not to push this too far, but life can seem to stretch before us like an ocean of soft plasterboard. If we want things to hold, we need to be aware that God is beneath all things waiting for us to fasten our lives into Him. As the letter to the Hebrews 10:22 (GNB) reminds us, "Let us draw near to God." How appropriate. In the language of a carpenter, to put a nail through a board into the underlying framing is to "draw them together." Indeed, He holds the whole world in His hands.

Not only knowing this, but living as though we know it is true is the essence of spirituality. As Paul puts it in Galatians 5:25 (NRSV), "If we live by the Spirit, let us also be guided by the Spirit." Unfortunately, that is not an easy thing to do. It is not easy to look at life through the eyes of faith and to get in touch with our spiritual nature. As one fellow put it, "I keep trying to get in touch with my deepest self, but I keep getting an answering machine."

So much works against us. We are incredibly busy people. Thanks to all those time and labor saving machines, we are able to cram event upon experience into every waking moment. We go at such a pace that days fly by like telephone poles on a country road. At this pace, how could one ever find a moment to experience God? How could we ever find a moment to pause and see the wonder of God all around us?

Unfortunately, our technology has taken most of the wonder from our life. Not much amazes us. Consequently, with all we have, with all we have achieved, with all we are capable of doing, many lead lives of quiet desperation. As the late humorist, Isaac Singer put it, "The second half of the twentieth century is a complete flop. The poor wish to be rich. The rich wish to be happy. The single wish to be married. The married wish to be dead."[4]

For most people, it is not that so much is really *wrong*. Rather it is just that not nearly enough is right. We have experienced so much and still feel a deep sense of emptiness. The old Peggy Lee song sums it so well: "Is that all there is?" Does life not have more to offer than to be born, grow up, work a lifetime, succeed, even accumulate some wealth, grow old, frail and die? Is that all there is?

Some would argue "Of course not. Life has mountaintop experiences. We have those moments of the spectacular. All of us can name at least a few." But people of faith need to respond that it is more than the mountaintop experiences that reveal the presence of God. Even the most ordinary events are filled with the possibilities of the Holy. Again Isaac Singer noted, "A writer gave me a story about a man with a chopped off head who could still talk. I said to him, 'Isn't it marvelous enough that a man with a head can talk?' "[5] And to that we can all add, "And sometimes it is amazing that those with head attached can not only talk, but make sense!"

That people can talk and sometimes make sense is not out of the ordinary. That does not, however, make it any less a source of wonder. We know the sun comes up every morning. That does not, however, make it any less amazing. Pause several times each day and through eyes of faith, examine the ordinary events. You will discover them filled with the presence of the Holy.

The essence of spirituality is to know that the whole world is in His hands and then to stand in continual amazement at the mystery of what might otherwise be thought the ordinary. That takes a very special way of looking at things. It means looking through the eyes of faith. The nineteenth century songwriter insists it takes a clearing of the senses: "Open my eyes, that I may see Glimpses of truth Thou hast for me; Open my ears, that I may hear Voices of truth Thou sendest clear; Open my mouth and let me bear Gladly the warm truth everywhere."[6]

The story is told of the minister who stopped by the hospital to visit a dying church member. This particular woman had led a long, good and faithful life, but was coming to the end of her days. The minister entered the room unnoticed by the woman. She was praying. He overheard her share with the Almighty, these words. "Thank you, God. It has been a wonderful trip."

Here was a saint who thoroughly understood that she had emerged from the ocean of God's love, had spent her time in the sun and was now preparing to sink back into the Ground of Being from whence she had emerged.

Would that as we all take this spiritual journey from birth to death we are that keenly aware of our God's presence —

as if we sense our wavelike nature as life rises out of the vast ocean of God's presence, moves across the water of time, only to fall back into the ocean of God's being.

The Indiana poet, James Whitcomb Riley says it a little differently:

> *What delightful hosts are they —*
> *Life and Love!*
> *Lingeringly I turn away,*
> *This late hour, yet glad enough*
> *They have not withheld from me*
> *Their high hospitality.*
> *So, with face lit with delight*
> *And all gratitude, I stay*
> *Yet to press their hands and say,*
> *"Thanks — So fine a time! Good night."* [7]

Indeed, He holds the whole world in his hands. To know that and to live as though you know it is the essence of spirituality.

---

1. Walter Brueggemann, *Genesis*, in *Interpretation: A Bible Study For Teaching And Preaching,* (Atlanta: John Knox Press, 1982), p. 22.

2. Kansas City *Star*, Focus section, February 22, 1994, p. 1.

3. Rabbi Michael Zedek, "The Spirit of Spirituality," an unpublished sermon, Rosh Hashanah, 1993/5754, p. 1.

4. Zedek, p. 3.

5. *Ibid.*

6. "Open My Eyes That I May See," Clara H. Scott.

7. "A Parting Guest," James Whitcomb Riley.

Proper 4
Pentecost 2
Corpus Christi
Genesis 6:9-22; 7:24; 8:14-19

Climbing Rainbows Through The Rain

The scripture lesson for this morning trips its way through the sixth, seventh and eighth chapters of the book of Genesis. This includes most of the account of Noah and the Great Flood.

For reasons you might or might not consider obvious, this part of the Bible generates considerable debate. From time to time, the controversy spills into the public arena. In February 1993, CBS had a two-hour prime time program titled, *The Incredible Discovery Of Noah's Ark*. The program, hosted by Darren McGavin, featured an archaeologist named George Jammal who presented evidence of having found Noah's Ark. He claimed to have actual wood from a "large ship" found atop Mount Ararat in Turkey. The program made additional claims to having evidence to prove a flood of world-wide proportions had resulted from subterranean chambers opening and letting water come to the surface of the earth. That is exactly as Genesis claimed it happened. The program went even further. It claimed evidence that biblical-era people had developed batteries for electroplating and even benefited from air-conditioning.

As one might imagine, this was a program to warm the hearts of all who take the Bible both seriously and literally.

"Imagine," the biblical literalist could now claim, "CBS, the network of Dan Rather and the liberal media, doing a program which proves the literal truth of the Scripture. Surely, this must remove all doubt that God is in the heaven and there is hope for the world."

Unfortunately, it was later revealed that CBS had been duped. George Jammal, the supposed archaeologist, was a phony. He made it all up. The piece of wood he claimed was broken from the ark was a chunk of pine he soaked in juices and baked in the oven of his California home.[1]

When those who take the Bible seriously and literally are made to look foolish, controversy is underway. At one extreme, those of a secular persuasion have their suspicions confirmed. CBS defended itself by claiming that they bought the program as entertainment and not as a documentary. Therefore, the program did what they wanted it to do.

On another part of the opinion spectrum, those who take the Bible seriously, but not necessarily literally, get very distressed when this sort of thing happens. The religious liberal points out that the Genesis account of the Great Deluge was never intended to be read as science. While all the Bible is to be understood as a statement of faith and not a claim of science, this is particularly true for the first 11 chapters of Genesis. Most ancient civilizations told stories of great floods. This account in Genesis is markedly similar to a Babylonian story called the Gilgamesh Epic. In fact, it is so similar that it can be argued the Hebrews simply edited the Babylonian story to fit their theology.

If you have ever read the account of the Great Deluge carefully, you know this perspective is convincing. Genesis 6-9 is not easy to take literally. This biblical account has significant inconsistencies. At one place it says that Noah took on board one pair of every species of animal. At another point he is told to take seven pairs of clean animals and one pair of unclean. At one place it says it rained for seven days, at another it rained for 40 days. It says that the flood lasted for 40 days, at another place for 150 days, and at still another it says the flood lasted for one year and ten days. It just depends on where you read. If you want to take the passage literally, which do you believe?

It seems that when we get to arguing about Noah and the Ark there are two mistakes we can make. We can be too insistent on taking it literally or we can be too insistent on not taking it literally. If we become extreme in either direction we are likely to miss a word of eternal truth. Let us say that you decide this must be taken as literal truth. In doing so, let us say that you find a way to harmonize internal inconsistencies by ironing out matters of how many animals and how long the flood. Let us even say you find remains of the ark in a glacial valley atop Mount Ararat. In and of itself, what have you accomplished? What difference would it make in your life? Would it make any difference in our world?

On the other hand, what would be accomplished by proving beyond a shadow of doubt that this is not literal truth? What difference does it really make that most ancient civilizations had flood stories? Does that mean Noah and the Ark is nothing more than a cute children's story? We can be so intent on demonstrating this is not literal truth that we risk making the terrible mistake of dismissing it as the eternal truth of God's word.

John Gibson is particularly helpful in cutting to the heart of things when he observes that even though this account speaks about something that happened in the past, it is really about the present.[2] If we really want to get from this story the message it has to offer, we should stop arguing about the issue of literal or not literal and instead, take the scripture seriously. Remember this is Holy Writ, and as such, tells us the truth about how God used to deal with human community and how God continues to deal with us. We need to take this seriously. This is God's word to us.

If we get to reading the passage instead of arguing about it, its authentic message begins to open for us. A central theme of the book of Genesis is that God had something in mind when he created the world. God placed very special creatures, human beings, in the midst of a wonderfully good world and gave them the responsibility to take care of it. God expected a marvelous relationship to develop between the Creator and the Created and God also expected a good relationship to develop between the people and the earth.

Almost from the very beginning, things start to go downhill. People proved to be bull-headed and stiff-necked. Like many a well-intentioned and caring parent, God is disappointed in the behavior of the kids. By only the sixth chapter of the first book of the Bible, God is so discouraged by human behavior that he decides on a total product recall. Particularly distressing is the amount of violence people have unleashed on the earth. God is so disappointed He wishes he had never made these people in the first place. God decides to handle the problem by wiping the human species off the face of the earth and trying something else. He had high hopes for humankind, but, obviously, it isn't going to work (6:5-7, 11).

In the midst of his despair, the eye of God falls on a fellow named Noah. He has been leading a remarkably righteous life in an immoral environment. God decides to reconsider his decision. Instead of destroying all humankind, God decides to show mercy to Noah and his family. In this very detailed account, the Lord God gives Noah instructions in front yard boat-building. Then comes the flood and the long wait for the waters to recede. Eventually, in a statement just beyond the limits of today's scripture lesson, God offers the rainbow as a sign of the renewed covenant between the Lord and His creation. The rainbow shall always be a reminder of the persistent caring of God; a reason to hope for sunshine in the midst of the rainy day.

Again this is not just a story of something from the past. This is an account of the present and the future as well. God had something in mind when He created us; something about the way we were to live, to treat one another, and to care for this garden we call the earth. However, things still don't always go according to God's plan. People are still bull-headed and stiff-necked. We still disappoint God and one another. We can count on it. When the human community fails miserably at fulfilling God's intention in creation, don't give up, for there are two things upon which we can count: 1) God will take some action to correct the matter; 2) and whatever God does, it will be tempered by mercy. This God continues to love us in spite of our behavior and He will not abandon us. Therefore, never give up hope.

If that is the script, we should prepare ourselves because things are obviously not going according to God's intention. God created a world in which moral laws may not be as certain as physical laws, but they are close. We might collectively decide that the law of gravity no longer applies. We can decide it has no place in this modern world because we have outgrown it. But if we step into an empty elevator shaft we will prove the law of gravity still applies.

In that same way, many today claim we have outgrown the Ten Commandments. We are modern people and don't have to concern ourselves with the superstitions of an ancient people. We think we know better than the Bible. We claim human sexuality should have no limits placed upon it. Greed has been classified a mandatory virtue for the successful American. Abuse of the public trust has become expected behavior for elected officials.

Twentieth Century America approximates the days of Noah in the prevalence of violence. A young man, only 21 years of age, is pulled from his ten-year-old car on a city street and shot dead so that two men, even younger, can steal his automobile — valued at less than $1,000. We should be shocked, but it has become commonplace. The newspaper reports it on an inside page of a back section of the daily newspaper under miscellaneous. We should not be surprised. After all, American homicide rates are four to five times higher, rapes are seven times higher and the rate of forcible robbery is four to ten times higher than in Western Europe. Is it any wonder that so many imprison themselves behind the locked doors of their own homes?

Contrary to popular opinion, we cannot blame it all on a lenient judicial system. During the 1980s we more than doubled the number of people behind bars. Presently we convict and imprison a higher proportion of our population than even South Africa or the former USSR![3] God intends us to live in peace with one another, but we are a terribly violent people.

A man abuses his wife. She retaliates by emasculating him. Rather than being appalled at the total breakdown of the covenant of love in that relationship, we sell t-shirts and use the trial as entertaining afternoon television. Each year we seem to move a little closer to the entertainment ethic of the Roman Coliseum.

Things are as out-of-whack today as in the days of Noah. This is not what God intended in creation. And just as in the days of Noah, when that happens, we can expect two things: God will bring judgment and moral corrective, and we can expect God to be merciful. Therefore, never give up hope for the betterment of the human community. That is the word of God which comes to us from this account of Noah and the flood.

Over 110 years ago a blind Scottish minister named George Matheson published a poem in a church magazine. Later it was put to music and has become the familiar hymn, "O Love That Wilt Not Let Me Go." The original third verse had the line: "I climb the rainbow through the rain." Matheson struggled sufficiently to feel as though he was trying to climb a rainbow.

Like Noah's rainbow, Matheson's was a sign of the eternal promise that God is still in control and refuses to give up on the world in spite of all the failings of the human community. Let us always remember that. Let us never give up hope. We can expect God to move in the midst of this immoral world. We can also expect God to be merciful.

---

1. William Tynan, *Time* magazine, July 5, 1993, p. 51.

2. John Gibson, *The Daily Bible Study Series: Genesis,* Volume 1, (Philadelphia: The Westminster Press, 1981), p. 176.

3. Paul Kennedy, *Preparing For The Twenty-First Century,* (New York: Random House, 1993), p. 304.

Proper 5
Pentecost 3
Ordinary Time 10
Genesis 12:1-9

The Risky Business Of Faith

Sometime between 1900 and 1500 years before the birth of Christ, a nomadic family, living on the socio-economic fringe of Mesopotamia and headed by a fellow named Abraham migrated from the fertile crescent of the Tigris-Euphrates River valley south through Palestine, eventually settling in the region of the Negeb desert. From one perspective, it was rather unspectacular. As Christians, however, we consider this one of history's most pivotal events. We believe that through a call issued to Abraham and his family, God fashioned a community to serve as a guide for faithful living that would result in a blessing for all the world.

For a moment, let us capsulize the message of Scripture to this point in Genesis. In creation, God intended a good world. He filled the world with creatures on which he could lavish all the love and affection He had to spare.[1] Unfortunately, things did not go according to God's plan. The most special of God's creation, human beings, proved to be a knotty problem. God made people a little less than the angels. That meant they had to have the freedom to choose whether or not to live as God called them to live. God took a risk in giving people freedom and it didn't pan out. People made a mess of things. They refused to live in harmony with one another or with the rest of the created order. They did not love and serve God. They did their own thing.

God, out of utter frustration, decided to wipe the slate clean and start all over again with Noah and his family. Another time, God frustrated an attempt to overreach human limitations by scattering the people and confusing their tongues.

In the twelfth chapter of Genesis, God decided on a different corrective approach. God established a relationship with Abraham and promised him that by his faithfulness, God would bless him and make of him a great nation. This status as a chosen people was to make Abraham a blessing to others. It was to be a relationship rooted in faith.

This involved a tremendous risk on the part of God. Human beings, after all, were the source of the problem. People were bull-headed and rebellious. People were the flaw in God's plan for a world filled with joy, peace and harmony. In spite of that, God gave the human community another chance. God decided to use the problem, that is people, to solve the problem.

We usually don't look at these things from the perspective of the Almighty. Our view is limited by our humanness. We think the option is whether or not we want to trust and believe in God. Actually, the issue is that God decided to trust and believe in us. In Genesis 12, God took a risk by giving people another chance. God, however, knew that to straighten out this problem, he was going to have to take some risk. Faith has always been a risky business.

That point can be made from the human perspective as well. To respond to the call of God and walk in the way of faith, the people had to risk. We are told Abraham was already 75 years old when God told him that if he would move to the Promised Land, God would make of him a great nation. Abraham and Sarah were very settled right where they were. Not only had they spent their entire lives in Mesopotamia, this had been the home area for generations of their kin. They knew all the neighbors. Abraham and Sarah had watched the local children grow into adults. They remembered when they were

32

little kids hiding in their mother's skirts. Abe had 30 years of perfect attendance at the Greater Tigris-Euphrates Rotary Club. Sarah served on the school board. Granted they lived as nomads on the fringe of Mesopotamian society. They moved from water hole to water hole. On the other hand, they were known at every oasis. It might not have been much, but it was home and it was comfortable.

Then this God named Yahweh called Abraham to take his wife and brother and go to Canaan. If they did that, this God was going to give them land to call their own and make of Abraham's descendants a great nation. "And in you all the families of the earth shall be blessed" (12:3), he is told.

Let us linger for a few moments and examine these details. Up to the day of his call, there is no particular evidence that Abraham ever heard of Yahweh. Although we cannot be certain, it seems reasonable to argue he had been practicing local religions. Why should he leave everything familiar to serve this new God? Certainly not because Yahweh made a particularly reasonable presentation. Yahweh, after all, promises Abraham that he will be the father of a great nation. However, Abe is 75 years old and doesn't have a single child. The thought must have floated through his mind that this God did not know what He was talking about.

What was there about the promise of this God, Yahweh, that attracted them? What would motivate a 75-year-old man whose family had lived in the area for generations to pack everything and move to an unknown place called Canaan?

We must conclude something significant was missing in their lives. Old Testament scholar, Walter Brueggemann, suggests the family of Abraham must have felt as though they had no viable future in Mesopotamia.[2] Their barrenness was more than childlessness. Their lives were empty. They were cut off from real meaning and joy. They had no foreseeable future, and cut off from God, they were without potential. They may have felt safe and comfortable in the Tigris-Euphrates River valley, but their lives were barren. To pump meaning into an empty existence they had no alternative but to step out in faith and go to Canaan. They had to leave security behind. They had to abandon the familiar. They had to trust God and step into the unknown. If they wanted a future, that was the only possibility. It was frightening and it was risky, but faith is always a scary, risky business.

The story of Abraham and Sarah is also our story. If you want to get out of this life all it has to offer, you need to risk leaving what seems safe, secure and comfortable in order to trust God and step out in faith. The scripture tells us they "journeyed on by stages toward the Negeb" (12:9). In that sense, we are always moving through some stage of life. Living is a continual journey. It is futile to think we can arrive at a certain place where everything will be safe and secure. We are on a pilgrimage from birth to death to eternity. We never get it all together. We never solve all the problems or remove all the dangers. Even if you arrive at a place called, "I got it made!" you soon discover it is not a permanent residence. It is only a rest stop on the road to whatever comes next.

Even if we somehow attain a goal of making life safe and comfortable, it is an empty, meaningless victory. For life at its best is an on-going spiritual journey toward loving God, loving people and serving the needs of others. To live any other way is to come up short. Robert Bly in his poem, "Snowbanks North Of The House,"[3] uses the image of the "great sweeps of snow that stop suddenly six feet from the house." Unless we risk and keep striving on this journey, we become like the boy who never reads another book after high school graduation or like the child who loses contact with the family and quits calling home. We are cut off from the past and have no tools to open a future.

For others, some event shatters the comfortable cocoon. The children are grown. They want nothing more than to settle back and enjoy life. Then one of their children dies. She was 33, but still their child. No pain surpasses that of burying one's child, no matter the age. They move through their grief in different ways and at different paces. They lose touch with one another. Before they emerge from the pain, they have lost their marriage as well as their child.

34

For others, it can happen differently. One night at a party, the wife sees her husband across the room and realizes she loves him no more. There was no problem, no crisis. The caring simply left. They took their marriage for granted and the warm glow of love drowned in neglect.

We are fellow travelers on this pilgrimage that goes from birth to death to eternity. We always move from place to place and stage to stage. It can be a frightening journey. Certainly it always involves risk.

The alternative, however, is not promising. To fail to take a risk can make us like the woman who puts down her rolling pin and bakes no more. We know people like that. For reasons not fully clear, they run out of enthusiasm in mid-life. By the age of 40 he has no other work-related goal than retirement. She no longer even dreams of an exciting vacation in a faraway place or even relishes a simple task like cooking a meal. Life comes up short. They failed to grasp that life is a spiritual journey requiring risk to move from stage to stage, step to step.

What a terrible thing when people give up on life. What a shock it can be to think you have it together only to discover there is always one more hill to climb, one more problem to face, one more crisis to endure. What a terrible thing to exist even for 70 or 80 or 90 years, but not to know the abundance of life.

To live to the fullest means accepting that we are on a spiritual pilgrimage. We don't have the option of comfort and security. God always calls us out of the present moment to risk moving into the future. Like Abraham, we always go by stages toward the Negeb. We don't know what comes next. We only know that our security is in our relationship to this God who will not abandon us. This is the God who is in Christ Jesus calling us over the tumult of life's wild restless sea saying, "Christian, follow me."

1. Gibson, Volume 2, p. 6.

2. Brueggemann, p. 116.

3. From *The Man In The Black Coat Turns,* (New York: Doubleday, 1981).

Proper 6
Pentecost 4
Ordinary Time 11
Genesis 18:1-15

The Oil For Squeaking People

Let me remind you of two biblical narratives which concern the announcement of unexpected births. In each case, the husband and wife are beyond the age when pregnancy is expected — yet the Lord tells them that a son will be born to them.

In the New Testament book of Luke, we are informed of how an old priest named Zechariah and his wife, Elizabeth, were to become parents of the fellow we know as John the Baptist. Zechariah was at work in the temple of the Lord in Jerusalem when an angel appeared to him. This angel blurts out: "You are going to become a father."

As an aside, let me note that the appearance of an angel is, even under the most ordinary circumstances, a bit unsettling to anyone. The news this angel offers nearly prompts a coronary to this old man, Zechariah. For he is told that his wife of the past 30, 40, 50 years is going to have a baby. The Scripture tells us that when he received the information, Zechariah was struck dumb and remained speechless until the child was born nine months later.

That reaction should not surprise any of us. We do not appreciate hearing that we are expecting about the time we have the golden wedding anniversary. The Scripture goes on to tell us that Elizabeth is so embarrassed at wearing maternity tops she doesn't leave the house for five months. Once again, that strikes me as a very understandable response to a difficult and unexpected circumstance. The condition of Elizabeth must have given the ladies of the local Bridge and Gossip Club plenty to talk about. Those nine months of waiting for the birth of John the Baptist must have been extremely difficult for Elizabeth and Zechariah.

In the book of Genesis, we are told of another unexpected birth to an elderly couple. In this case, however, they handled the news differently. Abraham and his wife Sarah were in the midst of a grove of trees when three strangers arrived and announced to Abraham that his wife was going to become pregnant and deliver a son.

Sarah was sitting inside the tent and overheard this announcement. It cracks her up. The Bible tells us she laughed at the news of having a baby at her age. Hence the child will be named Isaac which means "one who laughs."

Two birth announcements and two very different, but understandable reactions. Zechariah is struck dumb. Sarah laughs. Neither reaction changed the outcome. In both cases, sons were born nine months later. I do believe, however, that there was a marked difference in the ways Elizabeth and Sarah experienced their pregnancies.

Personally, I believe that Sarah had a much easier time of waiting than did Elizabeth. I don't have any "proof" of that. The Bible doesn't actually say there was a difference. My conclusions are drawn from my experience of life and a firmly held conviction that people in biblical times experienced their humanness in much the same way we do. I believe it was easier on Sarah, however, because she took advantage of one of God's greatest gifts — the gift of laughter.

In the face of an awesome surprise, she laughed. She applied laughter as an active ingredient to make things move more smoothly. As human beings we often find ourselves in very difficult, painful, squeaky-tight situations. Laughter is the

God-given oil, the lubricant which reduces the friction and helps us get through tough, tight problems. Laughter is a marvelous gift of a loving God and as such it is a gift we should carefully nurture and frequently use.

Consider how this gift assists us in learning. We must all learn it is evil to manipulate people. We should be straightforward and honest in our dealings with one another. People are valuable and not toys for our personal pleasure. Also, keep in mind that when we use people rather than value them, we pay a price.

Let me cast this lesson in the form of a story. A young 16-year-old boy entered the local pharmacy. He asked the pharmacist for three boxes of candy. "I want a two dollar box, a four dollar box and a six dollar box," the boy said. When the druggist commented that this was indeed a curious purchase, the fellow responded, "I have my first date tonight with a girl. I plan to take her to the movies. On the way to the show, if she permits me to hold her hand, I will give her the two dollar box of candy. During the movie, if she permits me to put my arm around her, I will give her the four dollar box of candy. And, if she wants to do some hugging and kissing, I will give her the six dollar box." The now-laughing pharmacist sold the boy three boxes of candy and sent him on his way.

That night the young man appeared at the girl's door. Her father answered and invited him in. "We are about to sit down for dinner, Jimmy," the father said. "Why don't you join us."

When Jimmy sits down at the table, the father asks him to say grace for the evening meal. Jimmy responds with a beautiful invocation in which he blesses the family and calls for a better world in which everyone treats everyone with decency and respect.

After dinner and on the way to the movie, Suzie, the young girl, comments, "Jimmy, I didn't realize you were such a religious boy. That prayer was lovely." To which the rather embarrassed Jimmy responds, "And I didn't realize your father was the town's pharmacist."

The lesson to be learned, of course, is that it is evil to manipulate people. We should be honest and straightforward. We should value one another. When we don't, it always catches up with us. It is an important lesson, but when given with a dose of laughter, it is medicine which goes down much easier.

Of course, laughter can be abused and abusive. Any of the gifts of God can be wrongly used. If we laugh to hurt people or as a way to avoid facing the issue, we abuse this gift. We should not, however, lose sight of laughter as a marvelous gift which strengthens and eases us through tough times.

For centuries people have recognized that, more than a pleasant pastime, laughter is good for us. Aristotle called it "bodily exercise precious to health." Carl Sandburg said, "Laughter is medicine for the soul." In keeping with the *Reader's Digest* feature, "Laughter Is The Best Medicine," scientific evidence has been added to the claims of psychology and philosophy for the beneficial effects of laughter. Apparently, laughter actually stimulates secretions from the endocrine system which reduce pain and stress.

In his well-known book, *Anatomy Of An Illness*, Norman Cousins tells how he treated a very painful illness by reading joke books and watching funny movies. He claimed that ten minutes of Laurel and Hardy film provided sufficient release from pain to get two hours of uninterrupted sleep.

Unusual? Exaggerated? Perhaps. Even probable, but still sufficiently true to make the point. Laughter is good for you. It improves the health and makes it possible to get through some tough times.

I am also aware that there is a darker side of human nature that hates laughter. Some people believe laughter sinful. Many humorless church folks claim it is frivolous. I contend, however, laughter is a gift our Lord Jesus Christ understood and practiced. Jesus, like Sarah, knew laughter can help ease us through an otherwise tight problem. Jesus frequently used humor to make a point or to lessen tension. When the Master spoke of such things as "a camel passing through the eye of a needle" or the need to "take the log out of your eye," his audience laughed. These words of immense exaggeration were spoken in tense situations. Laughter, properly applied, is the God-given lubricant to squeaky human relationships.

Some of what I say runs against the populist wisdom of the day. The experts currently encourage us to be confrontational with our problems. When angry with others, let them know. Be honest about your feelings. Tell it like it is. There is much to commend leveling with one another.

On the other hand, there is something downright demonic in thinking that we always have to confront every problem; discuss every difference of opinion; communicate to others every single negative emotion which flitters through the mind. God did not give us life as a problem to solve. Living is intended to be a joy to experience. One of the great aids for doing that is this capacity to see the humor and to laugh about some of the unfairness, the inequalities, the injustices that come to us.

Couples in troubled marriages usually spend an enormous amount of time and energy trying to solve problems and not nearly enough time and energy finding a few moments each day to laugh together. Maybe marriages are troubled simply because they have so many problems. Maybe people in troubled marriages don't laugh much because there is nothing humorous in their relationship. On the other hand, maybe couples who make a point of laughing together have just as many problems, but don't notice them as much. Maybe their laughter energizes them through the hurts.

Now I realize that sometimes things don't seem funny. It may hurt too much to laugh. Let me suggest, however, that may be exactly the time you need something to laugh about. To laugh when nothing seems particularly funny does not mean you are unrealistic. Finding something a bit humorous even in the midst of a troubled time doesn't mean you are avoiding the issue. We can see the humorous even when we are facing the issue squarely. Neither Sarah and Abraham nor Elizabeth and Zechariah were planning to have children when it was announced to them. After the golden wedding anniversary, we don't usually make those plans. For that matter, we never plan unwanted surprises. They come anyway. The choice is not whether or not tough times come. They will come. The choice we have is what we are going to do when the tough times arrive.

If you will remember, old Zechariah the priest met the problem with all seriousness and was struck speechless. His "take it all so seriously" attitude didn't change the end result. His wife delivered a nine-pound bouncing boy and they named him John. Between the announcement and the delivery, Zechariah was miserable.

Sarah on the other hand, decided to greet the news of her pregnancy with a bit of lighthearted laughter. Her laughter didn't change the end result. A son was born to her nine months later. The difference, however, was in how she experienced that wait. I suspect Sarah found the time of waiting much easier than Zechariah.

Quite frankly, that is one of the things we know about the value of laughter. It is the oil for tough, squeaky times. It is a wonderful gift of a loving God.

Proper 7
Pentecost 5
Ordinary Time 12
Genesis 21:8-21

When Life Doesn't Go According To Plan

The letter came from a college senior working as a student counselor in a dormitory at a distant university.

"Dear Mom," she began. "During my growing up years, few things irritated me as much as your attempts to quiet my righteous indignation by telling me that life is not fair. I swore I would never say that to my children. However, in my work with distressed college students, I find myself telling them the same thing. I still rail at life's inherent injustices, but I have learned I had best accept that unexpected and unwanted things happen. Life simply is not fair. Thanks for the advice I did not care to hear."

How universal this painful ordeal of learning that the world doesn't operate according to what we believe is fair. It happens to all of us and it has always been that way. This morning's scripture lesson offers a classic example. God called Abraham from the Tigris-Euphrates River valley and promised to make him the father of a great nation. Unfortunately, Sarah, Abraham's wife, was past the age when women normally have children. Since fathering a child is the logical first step in fathering a nation, other arrangements had to be made. At Sarah's urging, they employed an ancient form of surrogate parenting. Sarah suggested Abraham begin seeing her servant, Hagar. It seemed like a good idea at the time, but these things hardly ever work as planned. Down through the centuries, multitudes have thought they could engage in a relationship outside marriage without harmful consequences. Almost 100 percent of the time, people discover that monogamous relationships are difficult enough. An uncomplicated *ménage a trois* is all but impossible. Sure enough, things become problematic. When she becomes pregnant, Hagar ceases acting like Sarah's handmaiden and begins to act like the queen of the tent. Serious trouble ensues between the two women and Hagar finds herself out in the street. Things do not go according to plan. It took divine intervention to get her back into the house.

In time, Hagar delivers a son and names him Ishmael (Genesis 16). Things go relatively smoothly until 13 years later when Sarah conceives and bears a son of her own. This child is named Isaac. Abraham is now the proud father of two sons, one with his wife and one with his wife's maid.

The lesson for today opens about three years later at the traditional party to celebrate a child's weaning. Sarah sees Ishmael, now 16 years old, playing with his little brother. The boys get along very well. Isaac's little eyes sparkle when he sees Ishmael. Ishmael enjoys helping to care for his little brother. Sarah, on the other hand, harbors a deep resentment. The thought that the son of her maid stands to receive the same inheritance as her son outrages her.

Now it is true that she was the one who suggested Abraham have a child by Hagar in the first place, but that was before Isaac. Things just are not going according to plan.

Oh, how many of us have found ourselves in a similar situation. Something seems like a great idea at one point in life and a terrible idea at another time. I suspect many of the young adults currently succumbing to the fad of getting a tattoo will come to know precisely what that means. So many decisions made while young impact the rest of our days. Consider the people who are miserable at work. They chose the occupation for reasons which seemed reasonable, but by mid-life they changed or their circumstances changed and the joy that was once fulfilling is now a burden. Unfortunately, advancement, money and family responsibilities make it unrealistic to change jobs. Career choices can be as permanent as tattoos. Sometimes things just do not work out the way we want.

Sarah looks upon Ishmael as a tattoo, the permanent result of a choice she made under different circumstances. She tries for a course correction. She calls Abraham and demands that he get rid of Hagar and Ishmael. "Disinherit the boy and send them away," she tells her husband.

Abraham is shocked. He loves his son, Ishmael. Just because he has another son, Isaac, doesn't mean he loves Ishmael any less. I am reminded of a friend named Joe. He was raised by his mother and grandparents. His father, he had been told, abandoned him and his mother when he was an infant. As a young adult, Joe sought out and found his father. He had remarried, was raising a family and was living in the same city where Joe was attending college. Locating his father was a glorious experience. About the fourth visit, however, his father told Joe they could not see one another. His father explained that his new wife had not known about Joe's existence until he showed up on the doorstep. She was very angry. It was causing problems with his other children. The wife told Joe's father he could not continue to see this lost son if he expected to keep his happy home. He hated to do it, but he felt he had no choice.

Abraham finds himself in that same spot. He cares about both his sons as well as his wife Sarah. It becomes increasingly obvious that circumstances are such that he is not going to be able to have them all together. Sarah will not stand for it. Abraham must have mumbled about the inherent unfairness of life. He loves both his sons. He does not want to have to make a choice between them. Life is not going according to plan.

Fortunately, another divine intervention occurs. God tells Abraham that he should turn Ishmael out of the house as his wife requests. God will not only tend to Ishmael's needs in the wilderness, but Ishmael will also be the father of a great nation. To this day tradition holds that Ishmael is the father of all Arab people.

Consequently, Abraham prepares to send Hagar and Ishmael into the desert. To be perfectly honest, Abraham doesn't provide much for them. He gives Hagar and Ishmael some bread and one goatskin of water. For a trip through the desert this is not over-provisioning.

The text is quite fascinating at this point. It says that Abraham puts both the water bag and Ishmael on the shoulders of Hagar and sends them on their way. How curious! Ishmael is 16 years old and he rides off on his mother's shoulders? The scripture must mean that metaphorically. Hagar must have *felt like* she was carrying her son on her shoulders. That makes more sense. In fact, are there not parents here who feel as though they carry grown or near-grown children on their shoulders? Don't you wonder sometimes if they will ever grow up? Don't you wonder sometimes if they ever stop coming home in times of trouble?

It is the same from the perspective of Ishmael. Are there not 16-year-olds who feel as though someone else must carry them if they are ever going to make it? We don't plan for life to turn out that way, but life doesn't always go according to plan.

Hagar and Ishmael wander south to the wilderness near Beersheba. They exhaust the food and water supply. The strength of the teenager, Ishmael, fails first. His mother puts him under a bush, out of the blazing desert sun. As the boy sinks toward death his mother sits down about 50 yards away and waits for the inevitable. It is a scene as sad as those we see on the evening news. A famine in the land. A starving child waits to die. A mother sits nearby, her head hung in helpless despair.

Then Ishmael murmurs. God hears his crying. For the third time in this story, the Divine intervenes. Hagar opens her eyes and sees what seems to be an oasis. Could it be a mirage?

Perhaps, but waving palm trees in the desert stand out against the stark desert background. Hagar gathers all her strength and goes to see. Sure enough, it is a source of water. She fills the goatskin and takes it back to Ishmael. The water slakes his thirst. His parched lips are healed. He regains his strength.

This particular story ends by saying they continue to live in the wilderness. Ishmael becomes an expert archer. His mother finds him a wife from among the Egyptians who travel through the area.

There is a tendency simply to conclude by saying, "And they lived happily ever after." We might even want to say things may not have worked according to the *people's* plan, but they worked out according to *God's* plan and that is even better. Frankly, that would miss the point.

At several junctures in the story, God intervenes. Frankly, that doesn't solve everything. Sarah wanted her husband to have a son. She encouraged him to have one by the maid. God gave her the gift of a son, but she is resentful and bitter.

Abraham loved both his sons. He wanted to raise them both. When that plan didn't work out, God promised to take care of Ishmael and to make him the father of another great nation. But Abraham still feels guilty about sending Ishmael away. That boy was his own flesh and blood. Every time Ishmael came to mind, a pain shot through the heart of Abraham.

And do you think for a moment that Hagar and Ishmael were totally pleased with the way things turned out? Abraham had promised Ishmael half the family inheritance. They lost that and the life they had known. In exchange, they lived out their days in the desert.

Even when God intervenes, life does not always go according to plan. Life is not always fair. Any expectations that it will be otherwise are met with disappointment. We must come to terms with that. Life simply does not come with a fairness guarantee nor with any assurance that everything will work out.

We have plans about what we want to accomplish; what we want to accumulate; where we want to go. We may or may not attain those things. But even if we do, in the end, we discover it is not all that important.

The story is told about a Sunday school class in which a particularly effective teacher was relating the story of Abraham taking his son, Isaac, off into the wilderness to sacrifice him. The teacher told the story so well that one child covered his ears and said, "This scares me. I don't want to listen." Another child reassured him, "Don't worry. This is one of God's stories and they always turn out all right." Isn't that the point? You are one of God's stories and things will turn out all right.

A very committed Christian was desperately ill. She spoke about a recent visit she had with her aged and equally ill brother. She realized that this would probably be the last time they would see one another before his or her death. "In recent years," she said, "I have noticed it really doesn't matter whether we get together for a fun family reunion or for a sad funeral. Both events feel the same. It is not the occasion that makes the day. It is the loving relationship we have. Therefore, a funeral feels the same as a party."

That is the bottom line. What makes life go according to plan? Is it accumulating wealth? Achieving worldly success? Getting our own way? No, of course not. What makes life worthwhile are the loving relationships we make with God and one another. Everything else pales by comparison. This is the fact that makes a difference: You are one of God's stories and no matter how badly things seem to be going, you will turn out all right. Life may be unfair. Things may not go according to plan. No matter how many blessings God gives you, life may seem to come up short. You are one of God's stories and you don't have to worry about anything because you will turn out all right.

Proper 8
Pentecost 6
Ordinary Time 13
Genesis 22:1-14

When God Asks
The Unreasonable

Abraham and Sarah had longed for a child. Throughout their married life they had prayed to God for a son to be their heir. Thanks be to God, those prayers were answered. They were well past the age when one might reasonably expect the birth of a child when Isaac was born. How delighted they were. God had promised that Abraham's descendants would be as numerous as the stars in the heavens and with the birth of a male heir that promise was given tangible possibility.

In the scripture for today, Isaac is still a youngster when the Lord God speaks to Abraham and tells him to take his son into the mountains and sacrifice him. Can you imagine? Abraham is asked to kill his only heir, the promise in whom rests the people's future! We don't expect the Bible to tell us God ever makes such unreasonable requests.

The next big surprise comes when Abraham obeys. He takes his young son to the mountain and, without telling Isaac why, has the boy help gather the firewood with which he will become a burnt offering.

The story continues that when the sacrificial altar is completed, Abraham trusses the boy on it and prepares to kill him. Then as the father prepares to drive a knife through his son,

God speaks again. (To paraphrase) "Abraham, do not harm your son. I see that you are willing to be obedient and that will suffice. Instead of sacrificing your firstborn to me, capture a ram and sacrifice it instead." At that point, Abraham looks up and sees a ram with its horns caught in some bushes. He captures it and sacrifices it. The story ends by noting, "On the mount of the Lord, it shall be provided."

Now what in the world is the point of this story? How are we to make sense of God asking Abraham to kill his only son, his only heir? How are we to make sense of the scripture when it says that God did that to test Abraham? Are we supposed to believe that God might order one of us to kill our firstborn "just to see if we are willing to do it"?

To understand Genesis 22 it would be helpful if we had more information. Abraham's willingness to sacrifice Isaac is told without revealing the human side. In verse two, God tells Abraham to take his beloved son and kill him. In verse three, Abraham does. It doesn't say what went on inside the hearts and minds of Abraham and his wife Sarah. It doesn't tell us if she had input in this decision. And what about Isaac? Did he know what his father had in mind for that firewood? This passage of scripture has only a skeleton of facts. It doesn't give the feelings, texture and details we need to grasp the human drama and passion. This story is so brief we might call it the "Cliff Notes" on Abraham taking Isaac for sacrifice.

I suppose we must admit that there are any number of different ways to understand this admittedly troubling passage. The footnotes in the *New Oxford Annotated Bible* offer an historical perspective. It reminds us that "in its oldest form this story was told to show that the Deity surrendered a claim upon the life of the firstborn and provided an animal for a substitute."[1] It bothers us that God ordered Abraham to sacrifice his son as a "test" to see if he was willing to be obedient. However, in the ancient world, that was a common expectation of the gods. What makes this passage different is that Abraham doesn't have to do it. An animal suffices. As barbaric as it seems, it is really an advance over the common practices of the time.

We should not forget that the religion of the Hebrew people was radically different than that of the surrounding culture. Their religion was more than just an early belief in one rather than many gods. They believed in a God of justice; a God who was concerned for ordinary human beings; a God who cared. This was a radically different concept in the ancient world where the gods were thought cruel and capricious. We struggle with the unreasonableness of God asking for a sacrifice. However, in the end, God didn't require it and instead provided a substitute. That may, indeed, be the point of this passage.

Rather than the historical, we might look at this passage from a sociological perspective. From this viewpoint, we still sacrifice children. Thousands of children each year are victimized by abusive and neglectful adults. The fate of many children is determined by the parent who simply concludes, "I didn't want to stay married for the sake of the children. I decided I wanted my freedom."

Children are a gift from God, but unlike many other gifts, they are not intended for our amusement. Children cannot be treated as toys or used as vents for our anger. We have a responsibility for those lives. Parental joy emanates from seeing children learn and grow. Their lives are not ours for the taking.

Indeed, we sacrifice too many of our children. We no longer believe that the Lord God who created and sustains the world calls us to place our children on an altar and kill them, but we still sacrifice our children to lesser "gods." Every day children are sacrificed to the gods of consumerism, greed, indifference, violence. An innocent child dies in a drive-by shooting and we dismiss it as a trend of the times. Gangs of 14-year-olds shoot it out on the street corner and we accept it as part of the risk inherent in our constitutional right to bear arms. Indeed, we sacrifice too many of our children.

Rather than valuing our young, we treat them with scorn. The poorest class of people in this country are children. As some of the richest people in the world, how can we justify that there are children going hungry? As if it is not enough to sacrifice the present generation, we aim now at the future. Our worship at the altars of greed and irresponsibility has generated a national debt so enormous that our grandchildren will not have a choice as to how they want their taxes spent. They will be paying interest on our irresponsibility. The bumper sticker on the elderly couple's Winnebago in Yellowstone says it all. Indeed, we are spending our children's inheritance. From a sociological viewpoint, cutting a child off from the chance to make decisions about his or her future is to sacrifice the life of that child.

We might also look at God asking Abraham to sacrifice Isaac from a psychological perspective. Such a request seems terribly unreasonable, but sometimes we are asked to do the unreasonable. NBC's *Dateline* (7/20/93) featured the story of the George Keller family in Seattle, Washington. A serial arsonist was terrorizing the city. George Keller followed the newspaper accounts carefully and concluded the psychological profile fit his son, Paul. That didn't mean much until the newspaper ran the police artist's rendering of an eyewitness who saw a man running from the location of one of the fires. That drawing looked like his son, Paul.

The Kellers worried, thought and prayed long and hard. They concluded that they would go to the police with their suspicions. They did so because they were afraid that if they confronted their son and he was guilty, he would run. As it turned out their son was the serial arsonist.

Think about how hard that must have been for the Keller family. They loved their son, but they also knew that they had to do what was in that young man's best interest. They had to do something that was going to cause them and him a great deal of pain. In order to save his life, they had to sacrifice his freedom.

Every parent who has ever raised a willful child knows how difficult that can be. Every parent who has ever had to learn the lessons about "tough love" knows that God can, indeed, call us to do what seems very unreasonable.

I suspect there is something to be learned from each of the historical, sociological and psychological perspectives. It might also be helpful to step back and look at this passage from as broad a view as possible. There can be no doubt that asking a man to kill his son is unreasonable. On the other hand, let us not lose sight of the fact Abraham obeyed and God rewarded him with the life of his son. That I believe is the central lesson of this passage. As the old Gospel song states it, "Trust and obey, for there's no other way, to be happy in Jesus, but to trust and obey." It was totally unreasonable for God to ask Abraham to sacrifice Isaac, but the patriarch trusted and obeyed and discovered that God provided.

The lesson seems to be this. Many times God calls us to do things that seem unreasonable. We may like to think we know better, but we should just trust and obey. Step out in faith and do what we are called to do. I realize that runs counter to the cultural norm. We have this notion that everyone should think for himself or herself. We are so opposed to trusting the wisdom and authority of others that we really believe it when we say, "Well, that may be all right for you, but I don't believe that way. I am entitled to make up my own mind about what is true for me."

What nonsense. Theologian Stanley Hauweras observes that this notion that all of us should be encouraged to make up our own minds is suicidal. Most of us never learn how to think — period; let alone think for ourselves. As Hauweras puts it, we just don't have minds worth making up.[2]

In point of fact, we need to trust. Sometimes we need to trust that there are authorities that just might know more about it than we do. Certainly, we always need to trust God. And understand this. God will probably never ask you to sacrifice your oldest child, but God will call you to do some very unreasonable things.

For instance, most of the Gospel teachings are unreasonable. Jesus called us to love our enemies and to do good to those that hate us. Common sense says you should hate your enemies and do everything you can to destroy them. Our faith expects us to turn the other cheek when offended. We are to do that not once or twice, but 70 times 7. Common sense dictates that we might turn the other cheek once or twice but, the third time, we come out swinging. The culture teaches that greed is good. Get everything you can for yourself. Watch out for number one. Our faith has this totally unreasonable and unrealistic expectation that we receive when we give. That blessedness comes by extending a cup of cold water to the thirsty. That the way to receive is to give, not to take.

God does expect the unreasonable of us. And the way to the fullness of life is to do it. Trust God and be amazed at how he will provide. Trust and obey, there's no other way, to be happy in Jesus than to trust and obey.

1. *The New Oxford Annotated Bible,* New Revised Standard Version, (New York: Oxford University Press, 1991), Old Testament, p. 27.

2. Stanley Hauweras, *After Christendom?*, (Nashville: Abingdon Press, 1991), p. 98.

An Arranged Wedding, But An Intentional Marriage

Can anyone doubt the troubled state of marriage? Across the nation, we average one divorce decree for every two marriage licenses. In some parts of the country, as many divorce as marry each year. In spite of this high divorce rate, people do not give up marrying. In fact, a higher percentage of people marry today than a century ago.

It seems this problem can, at least in part, be traced to the high demands we make on marriage. Particularly, we have tremendously high emotional expectations. Our ancestors appreciated an emotionally satisfying relationship, but not as the first priority. They had more fundamental expectations. At the dawn of history, people married primarily for safety, not romance. In a hunting and gathering culture, the family was society's unit for physical survival.

As our forebears settled into communities, the family became society's unit for economic survival. While people still needed one another for protection and to insure propagation of the species, practical economic consideration was more important than emotional fulfillment. A husband and wife needed one another and needed children to make a living. If they happened to develop a caring relationship along the way, all the better, but that was not the central purpose of marriage.

Obviously, something has changed. We do not marry for economic or survival reasons. Men do not need wives to help with the farm. Women do not need husbands to support them. Today, people marry expecting more. We want our husband or wife to make us feel loved and appreciated. Today emotional support is the central reason for the relationship. If great-grandma and great-grandpa loved one another (in the sense that we have come to use that word), it was considered a wonderful added benefit, but not a requirement.

Obviously, all people do not need to be married. Multitudes live rich and full lives as single people. The point I want to make with this morning's lesson is that in order for a marriage to be satisfying, both partners must be committed to doing everything they can to make their partner feel loved and appreciated. Unfortunately, even that is not always enough. Some people do everything within their power to make their marriage work and it still fails. For many very complicated reasons, divorce is a continuing reality. It is not my intent to lay guilt or blame this morning on the divorced. My point is to stress the fact that without a mutual commitment to make a marriage work, it seldom, if ever, does.

Our scripture lesson for this morning provides details of a loving marriage that began with an arranged wedding in a radically different culture. I want to use this biblical story to illustrate that even after nearly 4,000 years, the principles which lead to emotionally fulfilling marriages have not changed. Whether the marriage is between ancient goatherders or modern stockbrokers, whether the engagement is arranged by the parents or announced by the couple, whether the bride and groom are subjects of the Bible story or they just happen to read the Bible occasionally, marriage provides deep satisfaction when husband and wife commit themselves to love one another and then do all they can do to meet the emotional needs of one another.

This particular account meanders through the entire twenty-fourth chapter of Genesis. It begins with Abraham worrying that his 40-year-old son, Isaac, has not married. Like an aging modern parent without grandchildren, Abraham decides to act. He summons his chief of staff and commands him to find a wife for Isaac. The servant must promise, however, that the woman not be a Canaanite. Abraham wants his daughter-in-law to be an Aramean, the racial stock from whence Abraham migrated many years ago.

There is good and bad in that. Modern research indicates that the closer in background a couple, the more likely a happy, satisfying marriage. That makes sense. Men and women are already sufficiently different to require many marital adaptations. The greater the other differences, the more adjustments. If you want to increase chances for a good relationship, marry someone with as similar a background as you can find.

On the darker side, Abraham's comment thinly disguises prejudice. Some of his best friends are Canaanites, but he doesn't want his son to marry one. How little things have changed through the ages. In the Balkans today people are killing one another. The Croatians and the Serbians are basically the same people. Both groups are Christians. They have lived together for so many centuries that many even have the same last names. However, Croatians are Roman Catholics and Serbians are Eastern Orthodox. Prejudice runs deep in the human heart.

Abraham's servant leaves the land of the Canaanites and goes to distant Paddan-aram to find an Aramean girl. He prays for God's guidance and establishes an observation post at the town well. A particularly beautiful young woman drops by to draw jars of water, and the servant concludes her beauty might make her a good candidate. Certainly, the servant must have thought, God would want Isaac to have a pretty wife. (Take note, friends, even in the ancient world, good looks was not a hindrance to finding a mate.)

When the servant asked this young woman named Rebekah for a drink of water, she not only gave him one, she volunteered to water his camels as well. Wow, she is not only polite and beautiful, she is also a hard worker. The scripture says the servant gazed at her in silence trying to discern whether this woman was God's choice.

Watering camels must be an enormously demanding job, for when she had finished, the servant gave Rebekah two gold bracelets, each weighing about five ounces. In addition he gave her a gold ring for her nose. Then he requests a night's lodging at her family's home. Again she complied. This young woman shows great promise.

The girl's father must have been dead because her brother, Laban, heads the family. When Rebekah and the servant go to the house, Laban catches sight of all the visitor's camels. He is impressed. The Bible does not indicate if Laban liked his sister's new gold nose ring. It does say that when the servant started giving expensive gifts to the rest of the family, Laban listened carefully to the marriage proposal. Particularly he shows interest when the servant insists God has led him to Rebekah.

As might be anticipated, Rebekah consents to the proposal. She gets on a camel and begins the journey. As they cross the Negeb Desert, Rebekah looks off into the distance and sees a man. It is Isaac. "Who is the man over there?" she asks (v. 65). For Rebekah, it is love at first sight. She is "thunderstruck."

As soon as they meet, they marry, as per the wishes of Abraham. The scripture tells us that Isaac falls in love with Rebekah, but it does not happen until later. In time, he loves her. The chapter ends with the simple statement that it is this relationship with Rebekah that comforts Isaac at the death of his mother.

Obviously, things were different in Canaan 4,000 years ago. Parents don't arrange the relationships today. The groom's family doesn't have to offer the bride a nose ring, a camel or, for that matter, a tattoo. Bride and groom don't marry the day they meet.

On the other hand, it is fascinating to see how many things remain the same. Like Abraham, aging parents still get nervous when the kids haven't presented grandchildren. It might not be gold bracelets and camels, but weddings are still expensive. Like Rebekah, some people still fall head over heels in love. If it is not love at first sight, then love comes very quickly. For others, like Isaac, real love takes time. For people today as it was for Isaac so long ago, a loving relationship can be a tremendous comfort in a time of trouble. It is also still very difficult to discern the will of God. Throughout chapter 24 of Genesis, people keep asking, "Is this what God wants?" And then, as usually happens today, the people really didn't know until later. God, it seems, seldom speaks clearly in the present moment. It is only in retrospect, as we stop to think and pray about it, that we realize, "That was the leading of God!"

While the scripture does not explicitly mention it, there is one other ingredient that has not changed. Marriage becomes emotionally satisfying when husbands and wives commit themselves to making one another happy. For the marriage to work, the couple must be intentional about making it work. Successful relationships are not built on a foundation of getting married to "see if it will work." People with good marriages commit themselves to doing whatever is necessary to make that marriage work. Even if the wedding is arranged, the marriage must be intentional.

That commitment has many dimensions. For one thing, it accepts that we marry a less than perfect person. As the Scripture says, "We have all sinned and fallen short of the glory of God." No mere mortal is perfect. In fact, after we marry we usually discover that some of the things we thought were strengths are really weaknesses. A woman remarked during marriage counseling, "When I married Dan, I loved his sense of humor. My family was so serious about everything. They never laughed. Dan had such a keen wit. Now I want to divorce Dan because he laughs at everything and never takes anything seriously." Good marriages learn to accept the frailties and weaknesses of one another. Marriages improve when husband and wife accept that every imperfection cannot be corrected.

Because of the imperfect nature of human beings, a really satisfying marriage will be committed to regular forgiveness. In any relationship, there will be times when a partner will hurt or disappoint you. There will be times when you will hurt or disappoint your spouse. It is only human for that to happen. For that reason, forgiveness must be a regular practice. If you don't forgive easily, you will clutch those hurts close where they will spoil and become like dangerous acids that eat away at your very heart. Be committed to forgiving easily and often.

We should also marry assuming the relationship will have its ups and downs. As the wedding vows remind us, we pledge to love one another in joy and in sorrow, in sickness and in health. We can be absolutely certain every extreme will be experienced before the journey ends when "death do us part." The roller coaster of ups and downs mandates we marry to make it work, not to see if it will work.

Another dimension of commitment involves striving to love whomever that person becomes. In a 25-year marriage the typical husband and wife undergo so many personal changes that it is like being married to three or four different people. As we age, we change. Our circumstances change. In order to be happily married, we have to be committed to love, not only who we are now, but who we become.

We make enormous demands on marriage today. We expect this most intimate of relationships to fulfill a significant portion of our emotional needs. Within the bounds of marriage, we want to feel loved and appreciated. We want to experience forgiveness. In marriage, we want to do nothing less than experience the presence of God. When that happens, it is not accident. For a marriage to work well requires enormous commitment and even more just plain hard work. Husbands and wives cannot take one another for granted. Love demands intentionality. But that commitment can be richly blessed by God.

Proper 10
Pentecost 8
Ordinary Time 15
Genesis 25:19-34

Don't Sell Your
Inheritance For Cabbage Soup

Paul, the greatest missionary of the Christian era, once remarked that God doesn't always use the wisest, strongest and most moral people to bring his message. Instead God uses the foolish, the weak and the lowly — just to prove a point (1 Corinthians 1:27-29). That truth certainly holds when it comes to those chosen by God as the patriarchs of ancient Israel. Consider our scripture lesson for this morning which concerns the brothers Jacob and Esau, children of Isaac.

With very little reading between the lines, we have to conclude that Isaac and his wife Rebekah from Paddan-aram had what today we call a dysfunctional family. Particularly note that their son Jacob was a mean, conniving, selfish, treacherous kid from the day he was born. In fact, Jacob was showing signs of an evil nature even before he was born. This patriarchal family is not composed of nice, conventional, moral, religious people. The point, however, is that God chose to work through and with this family. In today's story, God's purposes are entangled in a web of self-interested, self-seeking people. Yet God works to accomplish His task with Jacob, the "at-risk" kid and his dysfunctional family. As Paul observed more than a thousand years after these events, God uses the weak, the lowly and the foolish to make his message known to the world.

Listen to the lessons in this story. Isaac was the "late in life child" of Abraham and Sarah. When he became a man, he married Rebekah. It was not romance that brought them together. Rebekah was chosen by a representative of Abraham, Isaac's father, because she was of the right family, the right nation, the right age and in the right place. On paper, it was a great match. Isaac was a child of promise and Rebekah was of good stock. These two healthy people from good families married and set about to raise a family. Unfortunately, it didn't work out that easily. They were barren and had to rely on prayer and their faith in God for children. The lesson, of course, is that nothing has changed since then. Even with all our technology, advances in medicine and the help of the best child psychologists, we still must rely on prayer and put our trust in God if we are going to have a family and successfully raise that family. Children are, after all, a gift of God, not the result of scientific happenstance. Successfully raising children is always more a matter of God's grace than of good technique.

From the onset of that pregnancy, there were problems. Rebekah conceived twins and those two boys fought with one another even in the womb. About the ninth month of her pregnancy, Rebekah from that nice family in Paddan-aram blurted her frustration: "If it is to be this way, why do I live?" (v. 22). I suspect many is the mother who has made this same comment during a difficult pregnancy. In Rebekah's case, this only foreshadowed what was to come.

She had twin boys. Her first son was born with a reddish color and was given the name, Esau, which means red. The second son was said to have entered the world holding on to his twin brother's heel. He was named Jacob, a play on the word for "heel." The Bible does not provide an abundance of details from their growing up years, but it does tell us these boys were very different. The eldest twin, Esau, was an outdoorsman who loved to hunt and fish. As the eldest, he was also his father's heir. Esau was to receive twice the inheritance of his brother as well as the mantle of clan leadership.

Jacob, on the other hand, didn't like hunting and fishing. He thought putting worms on hooks and skinning rabbits a distasteful labor. Instead, he liked to stay home and help his mother around the tent. Consequently, Jacob was the favorite of his mother, Rebekah. She expressed that favoritism regularly. She even helped Jacob trick Isaac on the old man's death bed and warned him when Esau came looking for revenge.

Do you see what I mean when I suggest that we have here the makings of a dysfunctional family? They simply engage in too much undercutting and intrigue to raise healthy children.

As might be predicted, the kids have serious behavior and attitude problems. For instance, the Bible makes no attempt to conceal the fact that Jacob, among other things, is downright sneaky. He takes advantage of his old, blind father. He cons his uncle, Laban, out of everything from his daughters to his livestock. He outwits his brother Esau. There is a dark power at work in Jacob. He insists, grasps, exploits.

That, of course, is the focus of this morning's lesson. The twins are young adults. Esau spent the day hunting with his father. Jacob spent the day at home cooking stew. For lack of a better description, let's call it cabbage soup. Esau comes in from the field about 4:00 in the afternoon and he is hungry. The smell of that soup fills the tent. He asks his brother for a bowl, just to tide him over until dinner. Jacob offers a deal. If Esau will consign his birthright to Jacob, he can have a bowl of cabbage soup.

Several odors emanate from this story other than cooking cabbage. First, take note of the audacity. Those boys had no right to barter the family birthright. Law, tradition and Abraham made that decision. Again, this is not the healthiest of families and not the most mature of children.

When queried, Jacob establishes the price of a bowl of cabbage soup at the family birthright. Esau thinks for just a split second. "I am about to die (of hunger); of what use is a birthright to me?" (v. 32). Contrary to what he claimed, Esau was not on the edge of starvation. He was hungry, but he was not experiencing hunger. His stomach was not banging against his spinal column. He only had to wait two hours until dinner.

And so it came to pass that the birthright of the Hebrew people passed through Jacob and not his older brother. It happened because one man on one day didn't know the difference between "hungry" and "hunger." If he had only stayed hungry he might have had sirloin steak for dinner. Instead he settled for cabbage soup. Because Esau was not able to discipline present wants, he sacrificed future possibilities.

Unfortunately, people still do that sort of thing. A minister had a conversation with a fellow in his late 30s who expressed concern about his inability to earn enough money to support his family adequately. "I dropped out of college to get this lousy job. If only I had finished school, my life would be so different. This job has no future." That fellow's lack of present discipline cost him dearly. He sold his birthright for a bowl of cabbage soup. That happens regularly in a multitude of ways. Without present discipline, future possibilities are sacrificed.

Never sell yourself short. You have enormous potential. You are, after all, a loved child of God. That is your birthright and it comes with enormous possibility. Unfortunately, tomorrow's potential doesn't have much present market value. One of life's most demanding skills is learning to stay hungry today in order to realize tomorrow's possibilities. As much as we might like it otherwise, everything in this life doesn't happen when we want it to happen.

Learn to stay hungry in the pursuit of the worthwhile. Accept that you are not going to fulfill every material and professional goal immediately. Understand that most things worth accomplishing take time — many times they take decades.

Learn to stay a little hungry. It can make such a difference in your life. For one thing, stay hungry for knowledge. In fact, develop a deep hunger for knowledge. Too many people want to quit learning when they reach a certain age.

Don't do that. Keep on thinking. As the poet plans his life,

> *Let me die thinking.*
> *Let me fare forth still with an open mind,*
> *Fresh secrets to unfold, new truths to find.*
> *My soul undimmed, alert, no questions blinking.*
> *Let me die thinking.*[1]

Learn to stay hungry, not only for information, but for God. Unlike other institutions, we never graduate from Sunday school because we never learn all we need to know about our faith. Never let your beliefs harden to concrete. Be open to grow in your faith. You never know when God is going to confront you with a new idea and a new set of circumstances. When that happens, your faith can be stretched to such new limits it can never shrink back to the same size it was before. Stay hungry for God. Staying hungry now leaves us open to future possibilities.

Develop a deep hungering for life. Remember this truth: the best time in your life is wherever you are right now. After all, today is the only day of your life over which you have any say. Therefore, believe today the best and make the best of today. Life will, however, get even better wherever it takes you tomorrow, if you continue to believe that possible. God has created us in such a way that every age has its special problems and its special joys. God gives us the strength to deal with the problems as we encounter them. He also provides the grace to make the most of the joys. Don't wallow in guilt over yesterday. It is forgiven. Don't worry about the darkness of what is to come. There will be light enough to get through. Live in the fullness of today and stay hungry for tomorrow. What a difference that attitude can make. Having your life unfold day by day like a beautiful flower is your God-given birthright. Don't sell it for cabbage soup.

Because Esau couldn't wait for dinner, the history of Israel is traced to Jacob. In many respects, it is a sad, sad story. Obviously, Esau was no rocket scientist. Jacob constantly took advantage of him. Physically he never made it as a male model.

65

His entire body was covered with thick, red hair. I'm sure the kids in school constantly tormented him about that. His mother liked his brother best. This kid Esau had some serious problems. He had every reason to be a miserable failure in life. Surely any failure he experienced could be attributed to circumstances beyond his control. Hear, however, the rest of the story. Esau settled down in the hill country and raised a large family. Many years later, he ran into his brother, the one who had cheated him. Jacob was terrified that Esau would harm him. Instead, Esau threw open his arms and welcomed his brother. He retained no animosity over the incident. Esau grew up to be a loving, healthy man. He had his priorities in order. The Scripture tells us he died in peace.

In one sense, Esau sold a birthright for a bowl of cabbage soup. Jacob became the patriarch. On the other hand, Esau retained a far more important birthright. He was the loved and lovable, acceptable and accepted child of God. He never lost that.

Therein lies a wonderful lesson. Your birthright is the same. You are the loved child of God. You are worthwhile. Don't relinquish that gift. Circumstances may not be easy. You may have grown up in a dysfunctional home — like Esau. You may not be a particularly gifted person — like Esau. Others may take advantage of you — as they did Esau. Your mother may not like you. Rebekah didn't like Esau. You may encounter one problem right after another — as did Esau. But you are God's loved child. You are worthwhile. That is your birthright. You can rise above anything. Believe that and live as though you believe it.

---

1. "Let Me Die Thinking," Anonymous.

Proper 11
Pentecost 9
Ordinary Time 16
Genesis 28:10-19

Empowered By A Vision

If your mother taught you to say only nice things about other people, Jacob will push you to the outer limits of your imagination. This younger of the twins born to Isaac and Rebekah has few redeeming qualities. He takes advantage of every available weakness in others. The older twin, Esau, must have had the common sense of a fence post. On two different occasions, Jacob cheats him of his birthright. Jacob's father Isaac was old, blind and on his death bed when Jacob exploits the situation to benefit himself.

Jacob's father-in-law Laban tricked him into marrying Leah when he wanted to marry the younger daughter, Rachel. Later, however, Jacob got revenge by sneaking off with Rachel, taking many of Laban's household goods, as well as Laban's family gods. As Frederick Buechner says of Jacob, "He wanted the moon, and if he'd ever managed to bilk Heaven out of that, he would have been back the next morning for the stars to go with it."[1]

There just does not seem to be anything particularly likable about this man with whom God covenanted to continue the Hebrew nation. Jacob was, quite frankly, an unrepentant rascal! That's why we find today's story so fascinating.

Jacob spends much of his life as a wanderer. Like so many who live on the edge of trouble, his behavior mandates that he keep looking over his shoulder lest someone catch up with his shenanigans. On this particular occasion, we find him trying to stay clear of Esau. He has been such a rogue, he fears his brother wants revenge.

To avoid that, Jacob leaves Beersheba, where he has been living, and flees North to Bethel. It is an unsettled area, a place of desolation dominated by distant, craggy hills. Alone, Jacob arrives after sunset, carrying the few things he could grab as he left home. As the darkness settles in, he realizes he does not even have a pillow with him. In his haste to get out of town, he left it behind. He substitutes with the right size rock and lies down under the stars.

This wandering scoundrel might have been churning with guilt about all the mean tricks he has pulled on others, but frankly I doubt it. People like Jacob are much more likely to trace their predicament to the failing of others rather than accept any responsibility. "They got what they deserved. If they are so foolish as to let me take advantage of them, that's their problem." Any unpleasant thoughts Jacob had that night probably had little to do with remorse. Much more likely, he goes to bed feeling mighty lonely and with his stomach doing cartwheels for fear his brother might be gaining on him.

He falls asleep and dreams a vision at once awesome and disturbing. In the dream, Jacob sees an enormous ladder extending from the ground to heaven. Actually the image is not so much a ladder as it is a moving escalator. On this escalator are the angels of God and those angelic beings move up and down the escalator.

When Jacob fell asleep, he felt terribly alone. Here in Bethel, this place of desolation, he felt cut off from God and all other people. But now it has been revealed to him that he is not isolated. There is practically rush hour traffic between heaven and earth.

As his dream continues, the Lord God comes to stand beside him and reassure him. "I am the Lord, the God of

Abraham your father and the God of Isaac; the land on which you lie I will give to you and to your offspring; and your offspring shall be like the dust of the earth, and you shall spread abroad to the west and to the east and to the north and to the south; and all the families of the earth shall be blessed in you and in your offspring. Know that I am with you and will keep you wherever you go, and will bring you back to this land; for I will not leave you until I have done what I have promised you" (28:13-15 NRSV).

Jacob awakes inspired. "Surely God is in this place — and I did not know it." I will consecrate this as holy ground. And I shall never doubt that God accepts me and that God will care for me (28:16-19 paraphrased).

It was one of those awesome moments of *mysterium tremendum*. At Bethel, a place of desolation and loneliness, Jacob encountered the living God and experienced God's unconditional love for him. From that day forward, he was empowered by that vision. Whenever things started going poorly, Jacob remembered, "Surely the presence of the Lord is in this place. I can feel his mighty presence. The Holy is not distant. The traffic between heaven and earth is as heavy as the shopping center parking lot on sale day. Listen, I can hear the brush of angel's wings. Surely the presence of the Lord is in this place."

For hundreds of years this story has been a source of insight and inspiration for faithful people. We give it the shorthand of "Jacob's Ladder" and it is familiar as a song sung in Sunday school and youth camp. You might not know Sara Adams paraphrased the story for her very familiar hymn, "Nearer, My God, To Thee."

"Though like the wanderer, The sun gone down, Darkness be over me, My rest a stone; Yet in my dreams I'd be Nearer, my God, to Thee (v. 2).

"There let my way appear Steps unto heaven; All that Thou sendest me, In mercy given; Angels to beckon me Nearer, my God, to Thee" (v. 3).

It is said that the first verse was inspired by the story of a Christian martyr who was being mocked by a Roman soldier who was nailing the sufferer to a cross. "We will lift you a little nearer to your God," he jeered, only to receive the reply, "You are raising me nearer than you think."

We do not study the Bible, however, simply for historical reasons. The issue is not simply what that vision meant to Jacob and how his dream has been an inspiration to others. "What does it mean to us?" is the more fundamental question. It has important learnings for us to glean.

First and most obvious, how good to be reminded of the omnipresence of God. In some of the least expected places, we can be overwhelmed by the Holy. If it could happen at Bethel, it could happen anywhere. Indeed, God makes His presence known on the mountaintop of joy, in the valley of despair and in the prairie when the days stretch endlessly before us.

Jacob didn't expect to find God in the wilderness of his life and we don't expect to find God in the wilderness of our lives either. In the quiet times, in those moments when we are still and reflective, God's presence becomes the most obvious.

Unfortunately, so many of us don't take the time to be still and know that God is! We schedule every waking moment and maintain a breakneck pattern of busyness. Beneath the surface of our failing to discern the difference between important business and mere busyness lies a fear of being still. When we finally have a moment of quiet when we might ponder the meaning of the life itself, we fall asleep instead of listening for the brush of angel's wings.

"Surely the Lord is in this place and I did not know it," Jacob exclaimed. Maybe this rascal Jacob thought he was going to be as successful at running from God as he had been at running from Esau. It doesn't work that way.

A number of years ago, a prominent banker went to a professional meeting in Las Vegas. Since he was so far from home, he decided he didn't have to adhere to his usual high moral standards. Unfortunately, he appeared in the background on network television on the evening news going into a hotel with a young woman not his wife on his arm.

There is no place we can go to get away from responsibility for our own behavior and there is no place we can go to get away from God. For God is not only in Bethel, God is everywhere. And we are accountable not only in Bethel, but everywhere.

Yet another lesson from this passage of scripture has to do with the importance of an empowering vision. That dream of God's closeness to him and God's promise to him drove Jacob's life. It was the vision that sustained him during the hard times and inspired him toward being the person that God called him to be.

What was true for Jacob is true for people today. We are still empowered by vision. Everyone has a certain idea about who he or she is, what makes life worthwhile, what is important and unimportant. Collectively these beliefs form the vision that empowers our lives. Too many people, however, are driven by visions of the unimportant. They want to live for self. They don't include in their thinking anything about the difference between right and wrong.

Our faith offers an alternative vision for life. It has to do with the heavy traffic between earth and heaven and this God who is always near. This vision insists it is always better to give than receive, better to forgive than to seek revenge, better to love than hate. It is the empowering vision about the abundance of life that comes in Jesus Christ. That is the vision which forms a road map that can guide us the way we need to go.

One more lesson we must garner is always a disturbing one. It has to do with God's unconditional grace. Jacob is an unrepentant rascal and God loves him anyway. Jacob doesn't deserve that. He does nothing to earn it, but God loves him.

I am reminded of the story about the minister trying to find out why this fellow would never come to church. "Because I am just not good enough," the man explained. The minister attempted to dispel his anxiety. "Well, great King David was not a very good man either. He committed adultery and even murdered, and God still loved him."

"Is that right?" the fellow said, warming to the conversation. "A murderer and an adulterer? Well, at least I never actually murdered anyone."

Jacob was not a very nice person either and God still loved him. That is really the point of this story. As Frederick Buechner puts it, "God doesn't love people because of who they are but because of who he is."[2]

Indeed, it is by grace. God's love even for you is not dependent on who you are, but on who God is.

---

1. Frederick Buechner, *Peculiar Treasures*, (New York: Harper and Row, 1979), p. 57.

2. Buechner, p. 58.

Lectionary Preaching After Pentecost

The following index will aid the user of this book in matching the correct Sunday with the appropriate text during Pentecost. All texts in this book are from the series for Lesson One, Revised Common Lectionary. Lutheran and Roman Catholic designations indicate days comparable to Sundays on which Revised Common Lectionary Propers are used.

(Fixed dates do not pertain to Lutheran Lectionary)

Fixed Date Lectionaries *Revised Common and Roman Catholic*	**Lutheran Lectionary** *Lutheran*
The Day of Pentecost	The Day of Pentecost
The Holy Trinity	The Holy Trinity
May 29-June 4 — Proper 4, Ordinary Time 9	Pentecost 2
June 5-11 — Proper 5, Ordinary Time 10	Pentecost 3
June 12-18 — Proper 6, Ordinary Time 11	Pentecost 4
June 19-25 — Proper 7, Ordinary Time 12	Pentecost 5
June 26-July 2 — Proper 8, Ordinary Time 13	Pentecost 6
July 3-9 — Proper 9, Ordinary Time 14	Pentecost 7
July 10-16 — Proper 10, Ordinary Time 15	Pentecost 8
July 17-23 — Proper 11, Ordinary Time 16	Pentecost 9
July 24-30 — Proper 12, Ordinary Time 17	Pentecost 10
July 31-Aug. 6 — Proper 13, Ordinary Time 18	Pentecost 11
Aug. 7-13 — Proper 14, Ordinary Time 19	Pentecost 12
Aug. 14-20 — Proper 15, Ordinary Time 20	Pentecost 13
Aug. 21-27 — Proper 16, Ordinary Time 21	Pentecost 14
Aug. 28-Sept. 3 — Proper 17, Ordinary Time 22	Pentecost 15
Sept. 4-10 — Proper 18, Ordinary Time 23	Pentecost 16
Sept. 11-17 — Proper 19, Ordinary Time 24	Pentecost 17

Sept. 18-24 — Proper 20, Ordinary Time 25	Pentecost 18
Sept. 25-Oct. 1 — Proper 21, Ordinary Time 26	Pentecost 19
Oct. 2-8 — Proper 22, Ordinary Time 27	Pentecost 20
Oct. 9-15 — Proper 23, Ordinary Time 28	Pentecost 21
Oct. 16-22 — Proper 24, Ordinary Time 29	Pentecost 22
Oct. 23-29 — Proper 25, Ordinary Time 30	Pentecost 23
Oct. 30-Nov. 5 — Proper 26, Ordinary Time 31	Pentecost 24
Nov. 6-12 — Proper 27, Ordinary Time 32	Pentecost 25
Nov. 13-19 — Proper 28, Ordinary Time 33	Pentecost 26
	Pentecost 27
Nov. 20-26 — Christian the King	Christ the King

Reformation Day (or last Sunday in October) is October 31 (Revised Common, Lutheran)

All Saints' Day (or first Sunday in November) is November 1 (Revised Common, Lutheran, Roman Catholic)